MAMMALS of SMALL POND

Story and pictures by
Phoebe Erickson

Cover design by Phillip Colhouer
Cover illustration by Nada Serafimovic
Original illustration by Phoebe Erickson
First published in 1953
Originally titled *The True Book of Animals of Small Pond*
© 2019 Jenny Phillips
www.goodandbeautiful.com

This unabridged version has updated
punctuation and spelling.

Yellow Pond Lily

Mammals of

Pickerel Weed

Blue Fla

White Water Lily

Small Pond

For my friends of the Pond
Pop Wyble
Margaret and Haldane

Cattail

Arrowhead

WINDING BROOK
OUTLET OF POND

BEAVERS' DAM

BEAVERS' HOUSE

BEAVERS' SUPPLY PILE

SMALL

STUMPS OF TREES CUT DOWN BY BEAVERS

BIG MAPLE
RACCOONS' HOME
OTTERS' SLIDE
OTTERS' BURROW
MINKS' BURROW
POND
Feeding PLATFORMS
WINDING BROOK
MUSKRATS' HOUSE
MARSH
INLET TO POND
MUSKRATS' BURROW
UNDER BANK)
TINY STREAMS FLOWING INTO POND

WINTER

The Mink slipped out of his burrow near the edge of Small Pond. He sniffed the cold air. Then he turned to see what was stirring the dried leaves.

A plump Raccoon waddled past. She had just crossed the frozen marsh. But she had found no food. The frogs and the clams and the turtles were buried deep in the mud. The grubs and the worms were hidden in the frozen ground.

The Raccoon was ready for her long winter sleep. She climbed the rough trunk of a big maple. Her winter home was in a deep hollow in the trunk of the tree. When she reached the opening, she squeezed her fat, furry body into it and

climbed down to her nest below. Soon she was fast
asleep.

The Mink was hungry. He slipped through the
dry marsh grass until he reached the Beavers' Dam
at the far end of Small Pond. There he saw some
fish swimming under the ice. At first he thought
he could catch them. The ice looked thin, but he
couldn't break through it.

Just then, the Otter climbed up on the Beavers'
Dam. He sat very still, watching the Beavers
swimming under the ice. Fish swam past the
Beavers who paid no attention to them. But the

Otter trembled. All those fine fish and no way to get at them!

The ice had locked the Beavers into Small Pond. They swam back and forth inspecting their dam. One of them dived to the bottom and brought up clumps of mud and roots. They patted and poked it into the side of the dam.

The Beavers had made Small Pond by building

their dam across Winding Brook. The dam held the water back and flooded the valley. The Beavers needed deep water to keep their store of poplar, alder, birch, and willow branches fresh and green. They lived on the bark from these trees.

Small Pond became a home for many birds and fish and animals. It made a moist place for plants and trees to grow. It kept the rich soil from being carried away by the swift waters of Winding Brook.

When the Beavers were sure that their dam was strong enough to hold against the ice, they swam away. Their house was near the middle of Small Pond. Next to it was their pile of branches. It was held to the bottom of the pond with stones and mud.

Each Beaver took a branch. They entered their house through an underwater passage. It led up to a large room which was above water level. The walls and ceiling were made of sticks and mud. Tiny holes let in fresh air.

When the Beavers had finished their meal, they

took the bare branches out and added them to the outside walls of their house. That made the house larger and stronger.

The Muskrat caught a small fish. The other Muskrat nibbled at the stem of a water plant. Then she found a clam. They swam to their home in the marsh.

The Muskrats' house was made of mud and
rushes and cattail stalks. It was very much like
the Beavers' house, only smaller. Two underwater
passages led to a dry room at the top. Here the
Muskrats ate and slept. Fish bones and clam shells
were scattered about. They weren't as neat as the
Beavers. When they had eaten the fish and the
clam, the Muskrats went to sleep on a bed of dried
rushes.

The Muskrats didn't store up food for the winter.
If fish and clams and water plants were scarce, they
ate some of the roots and stalks that formed the
walls of the house.

The snow made a soft hissing sound on the ice

that covered Small Pond. Under it, the Beavers and the Muskrats were safe and snug. They had nothing to do but eat and sleep until spring.

The ice locked the Mink and the Otter out of Small Pond. Even Winding Brook was frozen over, but the Otter heard the water tinkling. He followed its sound until he came to the rapids. There he found a place to get under the ice. In a deep, muddy hole, he caught a crayfish and swam back to the opening. He was just in time; a thin sheet of ice had covered it. The Otter broke through it and climbed up on the bank to eat the crayfish. Soon he was on his way to the Big River.

Snow drifted and swirled through the forest.

The Mink was following a fresh rabbit trail, but when a mouse ran out, he jumped on it. Next he caught a shrew. By this time the rabbit's trail was lost under the snow.

The Mink knew that all animals would look for shelter from the storm. So he edged under a big rock and sniffed around. A hissing snarl made him jump back. He had almost bumped noses with the Otter!

The Mink was a scrappy fighter, but he was no match for the Otter. He scurried away and found

a deep hole under a stump. There he curled up and
went to sleep.

The Otter came out of his shelter under the
rock. It had stopped snowing. He plowed through
the drifts and at last came to Big River. Only the
edges of the swift flowing river were frozen. The
Otter slipped and slid down the steep bank.

SWOOSH—he went, and then SPLASH! into
the river. The cold running water felt very good
to the Otter. He dived and splashed for a while
and then swam upstream. Into the other bank, he
found the underwater entrance to a burrow. It had

once belonged to a Muskrat. Last year the Otter had dug it out until it was large enough for him to squeeze through. He followed a long tunnel that led up to the burrow.

A family of field mice scampered out. The Otter was too tired to try catching them. He slept for a long time. When he went back to fish in the river, moonlight made a sparkling path on the water.

The Mink woke up and shook the dried leaves from his coat. Moonlight flooded the forest. He bounded away toward the Big River. There he

found a burrow under the roots of a pine tree. But the Mink was too restless to stay in one place all winter. He went on long trips through the forest, hunting for game. When he fished in the river, he saw the Otter.

A deep blanket of snow covered Small Pond. The Beavers' house and the Muskrats' house were small white humps. The Raccoon slept in her nest in the big maple tree. Sometimes when she was half awake, she heard a fox barking at the moon.

SPRING

Tap-tap-tap! A woodpecker beat at the bark of the big maple tree.

The sound awakened the Raccoon. She opened her eyes and yawned. Then she climbed to the opening and made her way down the trunk of the tree. She had been out before, but this time the air felt different. It was warmer, and she could hear the brook.

A strong west wind ruffled her fur as she
waddled through the melting snow. She was very
thin and very hungry. At the edge of Winding
Brook, she dug into the mud with her slender
paws. All she found were a few grubs and snails.

Rain fell and melted the snow. One day, the
Beavers heard a loud snapping and cracking in the
ice above them. Spring had come, and the ice in
Small Pond was breaking up.

The Beavers hurried to their dam. Big pieces of

ice were pushing against it. Some of the sticks and mud were torn loose. The Beavers were worried, but there was no time to lose. They climbed up on the bank to look around for sticks and fallen branches. One of them began to gnaw at the trunk of a tree.

Beavers' teeth are sharp and strong. At last the tree began to tremble. Then it fell with a crash. They cut off the branches and gnawed the long trunk into pieces. It was hard work. They puffed and grunted and pushed and pulled.

While the Beavers were working, the ice piled up against the dam. Suddenly, it broke through,

and the swift flowing water hurled the ice into
Winding Brook below. The Beavers heard the
sound of the rushing water. They dived into the
pond to see what had happened. There was a wide
break in the dam.

The Beavers swam back to the bank. They
dragged down more sticks and branches and cut
down more trees. When the ice had passed, they
would start to repair their dam.

The Muskrats felt their house wobbling! They
hurried down the passageway and into the pond.
Rain splashed on the patches of open water.

Wind beat at the reeds and pushed blocks of ice against the sides of their house.

During the winter the Muskrats had eaten many of the roots and stalks of which it was made. Now the walls were thin and shaky. Suddenly, a big piece of ice swept its top away. Fish bones and clam shells were tossed into the water.

The Muskrats dived. They swam through a long tunnel which they had dug under the bottom of Small Pond. The tunnel led to burrows deep in the bank. In the summer the Muskrats used these tunnels as hiding places.

The burrows were lined with dried grass and rushes. Several passages led back to the pond. The Muskrats lived in these burrows for a long time.

More rain fell, and the marsh turned slowly green. Ducks and birds came back from the south. Now and then a frog croaked in a deep voice. At night the peepers called.

When the ice broke up, the Mink and the Otter came back to Small Pond.

One day, the Mink was hunting for frogs in the marsh. He saw a large bass and streaked after it. The fish headed for deep water. After taking a quick gulp of air, the Mink dived. Down and down he went and hid among some water plants. Soon he saw the bass. It was swimming slowly, moving its tail gently back and forth. The Mink waited, his beady eyes gleaming.

The big shell of a snapping turtle moved in the mud below. It poked its head out from its shell and began to swim up. With a flip of its tail, the bass made a wide circle. The Mink shot out.

But the water swirled around him. He saw the long, dark body of the Otter flash past. After a few

twists and turns, the Otter caught the bass and swam back toward the shore.

The Mink was very angry, but he wasn't big enough to fight the Otter. He shot up to the surface of the pond and took a deep breath. He had been underwater for a long time.

The Beavers were repairing their dam. First, they fitted sticks and poles and branches into the break made by the ice. Then, they brought up stones and mud from the bottom of the pond.

The Beavers used their front paws to pat the mud into place. They knew just how high to build the dam to keep the water in Small Pond at the right level.

One of the Beavers climbed up on the bank to get a long pole. He pushed and puffed and pulled. A loud WHACK! WHACK! from the pond made him jump. He ran as fast as he could on his short legs and dived into the water.

The other Beaver had heard a strange noise. She
had warned him of danger by slapping the water
with her broad, flat tail. As they swam away, they
saw a fox on the far bank.

The days grew warmer. Stalks and water plants
sent up new green shoots. Nesting birds twittered
in the marsh. One night, the whip-poor-will called
in clear mellow notes.

Strange sounds came from the Beavers' house. Two tiny baby Beavers chattered and squealed in their nest of soft, dry grasses.

In the burrow deep in the bank, four baby Muskrats crawled about.

Three little Raccoons played together. They were safe in their nest in the big maple tree.

The Mink and the Otter had families too. Three little Minks lived with their mother in a burrow near Small Pond.

A deep hole between two rocks was the home of the new baby Otter.

Summer

The two baby Beavers had just had their first swimming lesson. Now they were lying in the warm sun on the top of their house. The big, flat lily pads began to rock, and the Otter's head poked out of the water.

WHACK! went the mother Beaver's tail.

The little Beavers slid into the pond. Their
webbed hind feet pushed out and down they went.
The mother Beaver hurried them up the passageway
and into the house. She didn't trust the Otter so
near her babies.

Beavers like to keep the inside of their house
dry. The little ones squeezed the water from their
fur with their tiny paws. The water ran down the
entrance hole. When they were fluffy and dry, they
rolled and tumbled together on soft beds of rushes.

There were four beds—one for each Beaver. They were careful to keep them clean and neat.

The mother Raccoon brought her three babies down the trunk of the big maple tree. With a low "chirr," she warned them to keep quiet. At the edge of Small Pond, she found grubs and snails for them to eat.

The little Raccoons poked around in the mud. One of them caught a frog, but it got away. Then they all fought over a white pebble. The mother Raccoon found a large clam. She opened the shell with her sharp teeth. After washing the sand from

it, she gave it to the little ones. Then she found some food for herself.

The father Muskrat started to repair their old house in the marsh. When their babies were old enough to be left alone, the mother Muskrat helped him. They used their sharp teeth to dig up clumps of mud and roots and cattail stalks. When the pile was well above the water, they hollowed out a large room at the top. Two tunnels led out to the pond. It was really a fine new house—much bigger and stronger than the old one.

But the baby Muskrats didn't like being left in the burrows. One day, they followed their mother down the tunnel toward the pond. When they reached the water, they began to squeak and squall. The mother Muskrat led them back to the burrow, but they followed her again. At last, she grabbed one baby in her teeth. She swam out to the pond and put him on top of the new house. The father Muskrat watched while she went back for the others. When they were all safely out, she gave them some clam shells to play with.

The mother Otter and her baby were playing
in the grass at the edge of Small Pond. When the
little one climbed on her back, she slipped into the
shallow water. Round and round she swam. Then
she rolled over. The baby Otter slid into the water.

At first, he didn't like that at all. He scrambled
toward the shore, making little whimpering sounds.
But the mother Otter coaxed him into trying it
again. This time, he swam a few strokes. Soon he was
swimming all by himself. In time he learned how to
dive and how to catch fish and frogs and turtles.

The three baby Minks snapped and snarled at each other. They were fighting over a fish which their mother had brought them. She growled at them, but they paid no attention. At last she pushed them apart, and they finished their meal. After a nap, they played in the shallow water at the edge of the pond. When the mother Mink swam into the pond, the little Minks followed her. They were not afraid of the water and soon learned to swim. In a few days, they were trying to catch fish and frogs. They were almost too busy to fight.

When the little Beavers were hungry, they squeaked and squealed. The mother Beaver gave them some tender leaves to eat. Then she brought up a branch and showed them how to gnaw the green bark. At first their tiny teeth just scratched the bark, but they liked the taste of it.

When the little Beavers had learned how to swim, the mother Beaver taught them how to dive and slap the water with their tails. Sometimes they kept watch while the father and mother Beaver were working.

The four baby Muskrats climbed on the mother Muskrat's back. She swam in and out among the rushes. One by one, the little ones slipped into the water and pushed out with their webbed hind feet. At first they bumped into reeds, but they soon learned how to steer themselves with their long tails.

They grew very fast. Before long, they were helping to build islands of mud and roots in the marsh. From the tops of these islands, the Muskrats could see in all directions. They used them as feeding places. If an enemy came near, they dived into the water.

Pond lilies opened wide to the hot summer sun. Red-winged blackbirds flashed in and out of the marsh. "Ok-a-leek-ok-a-leek," they called.

Autumn

Frost nipped at the leaves. Red and yellow and orange, they floated down and rested on Small Pond.

The three young Minks scurried through the woods. The mother Mink was teaching them how to hunt. She dug at a rotted stump. A family of mice dashed out. The young Minks scrambled after them.

The father Mink didn't live with his family. But when they left Small Pond to find homes of their own, he came back to the old burrow.

Splash! Splash! Splash! The three Otters came sliding down a steep bank. They dived head first into Small Pond. Water ran from their sleek coats as they climbed the bank and came down again. They played this game for a long time. Then the father Otter swam off and came back with a fish. They shared the meal.

The young Otter was almost grown up, but he stayed with his family. They played and fished and went on trips to other ponds and streams.

The four young Muskrats were grown up. They were building houses of their own. The father and mother Muskrat helped them. One of the Muskrats sat on a feeding island while the others worked. He was watching and listening. Suddenly, he saw a big ripple. Then the sleek head of the Mink rose above the water. The Muskrat dived. Whack! went his tail on the water. The other Muskrats heard his warning and dived. They all swam into their tunnels under the bottom of Small Pond. The Mink didn't find them.

The Muskrats covered their houses with stalks and leaves and marsh grass. They would need some of this as food during the winter.

The Beavers were getting ready for winter. They
strengthened their dam and added fresh mud and
sticks to the outside walls of their house. They cut
down trees and floated the branches out to their
supply pile. When Small Pond was frozen over,
they would eat the green bark from the branches.

The young Beavers helped. They were almost
grown up, and next year they would build houses of
their own.

Cold north winds whistled through the bare trees. Thin fingers of ice reached out from the edges of Small Pond.

The Raccoon shuffled through the fallen leaves. She dug some grubs from a rotted log. Frost-blackened wild grapes hung from a vine. She rested against the log and ate them greedily.

Under the Raccoon's heavy fur was a thick layer of fat. She would need this fat to keep her warm during her long winter sleep.

The three young Raccoons hunted by themselves. Sometimes they came back to the nest in the big maple tree. The Raccoon yawned. She too would soon climb up to the nest for the winter.

Again, snow and ice covered Small Pond. Under it, the Beavers and the Muskrats were snug in their houses. The Mink and the Otter went to the Big River. High up in the maple, the Raccoon and her family slept soundly.

The End

About this story...

The pond in this book is just beyond Phoebe Erickson's home near New Milford, Connecticut.

Often she went out at dawn in her rowboat to sketch the little animals: the beaver, the muskrat, the raccoon, the mink, the otter. It is the beavers' pond. They made it by damming up the brook. They guard their dam against the ravages of ice and weather. They maintain the pond and so provide a home for the other animals.

This true account of the animals of Small Pond follows the seasons from the time the pond first freezes over until summer is gone again and the babies are raised.

More Books from The Good and the Beautiful Library!

Brian's Victory
by Ethel Calvert Phillips

Mpengo of the Congo
by Grace W. McGarran

David and the Seagulls
by Marion Downer

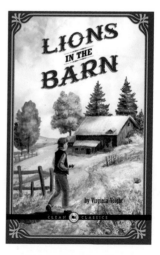

Lions in the Barn
by Virginia Voight

www.goodandbeautiful.com